Typesetting © Veneficia Publications UK
VENEFICIA PUBLICATIONS UK
veneficiapublications.com

# THE PROMISE OF DAWN:

## Rites of Passage for all Beliefs

# Patricia Sumner

*Sumner*

*To Rhian,*
*Best wishes,*
*Pat*

# CHAPTERS

# INTRODUCTION

It has been an honour and a privilege to write this 'Rites of Passage' collection for Veneficia Publications. I was delighted to be asked by Diane Narraway to compose readings and poems to commemorate the significant milestones in our lives – though, I have to admit, I have felt unqualified for the task.

I studied English Literature and Philosophy many years ago, particularly enjoying the 'Philosophy of Religious Belief' element of the degree course. Today, I still read all kinds of literature relating to spirituality, the religions of the world, theology, and philosophy. It's what makes me tick – this and my love of creative writing.

The spiritual dimension has always drawn me. I feel there is much more to life than we can measure, touch, or fully understand. I probably feel this way due to the profoundly spiritual experiences I have had, especially following the death of a loved one.

I enjoy my deepest moments of spiritual connection when immersed in nature (and this is a recurring theme in the collection). I believe that all of life is sacred; that the same life force or spirit flows through each one of us – every person, animal, plant, and stone – and I rejoice in nature's seasons and cycles. If life is viewed as sacred, then every act of living becomes a religious act, and the protection of the planet becomes paramount.

I also believe in the power of community. As social beings, we're not meant to be alone – at least not for prolonged periods. We need to come together to celebrate life's major events, to create memories, and to make meaningful connections with others – though 'others' could include the animals and plants of our natural environment or even the global community of manifold peoples.

For much of my life, I have attended Church in Wales services. I feel particularly in tune with Celtic Christianity (i.e., finding spirit in nature) and I respect and hold dear the teachings of Jesus. I also have a great deal of sympathy for Buddhism, accepting the possibility of reincarnation and appreciating the benefits and power of meditation. However, I think it is the Golden Rule of all the great faiths that appeals to me the most: "So in everything, do unto others what you would have them do to you, for this sums up the Law and the Prophets" (Matthew, 7:12). This Golden Rule is expressed in one form or another in most religions, and it has taught me that compassion, forgiveness, tolerance, equal rights for all, humility and kindness should be our guiding principles – and all these principles can be expressed simply as 'love.'

Ultimately, of course, we must all find our own path, and I want to stress that you don't have to adhere to a particular religion or philosophy to enjoy this collection of readings. 'The Promise of Dawn' has been designed for anyone – and especially for those of no specific denomination, or no faith at all. Many of us find the concept of 'God' to be complex and problematic. Therefore, you won't find the word 'God' in the following pages, or any mention of the Prophets. However, I hope the following readings will resonate with you, and you will find meaning and comfort during life's highs and lows.

Finally, I'd like to say that the material in this book amounts to ideas and suggestions only; please take whatever moves you and make it your own. Use it in your own creative ways, perhaps to form the basis of a ceremony or to personalise a celebration according to your own tastes. We all have different outlooks on life and spirituality; there's no single correct way. Therefore, the contents of this book are not meant to be a new kind of doctrine or prescribed text. Instead, pick and choose readings, as you see fit, crafting a tribute that feels right for you and your loved ones, or simply finding solace in the poems during times of solitude. My sincere hope is that 'The Promise of Dawn' will raise questions, stir emotions, and maybe even spark moments of wonder, connection, and love.

Wishing you well on your journey,

Pat

## CHAPTER 1
## BIRTH AND NAMING CEREMONIES

*"Stop acting so small. You are the universe in ecstatic motion." – Rumi*

## BEARING WITNESS
*(Use name in place of 'little one' if preferred)*


We call upon the winds of the north, south, east,
and west,
on the warm, moist earth and gentle rain,
on raging fire and flowing mountain streams
to bear witness to this momentous day.

We call upon the birds of the air,
the raven, hawk, swift, and woodpecker,
and the mammals of this precious land –
otter, fox, hedgehog, and badger.

We call upon the animals of the deep,
the starfish, bass, eel, and porpoise,
and the small creatures that live among us –
ants, beetles, bees, and moths.

We call upon nature itself:
the invisible code held tight within an acorn
urging it to reach a great oak's heights,
water's relentless downward journey
on hearing the distant ocean's cry.

We call upon our ancestors,
loved ones who have gone before us,
over many generations and in many lands;
we feel your comforting presence
as we gather before you now.

And we call upon you who are present here today
to welcome this new young life,
this miracle of creation
into our arms and into our midst.

We have waited for you, _little one._
With bated breath and excitement,
we have anticipated
your first moments on this earth.

We acknowledge you,
celebrate your beating heart,
small limbs, and curious brain,
that beautiful, bright-eyed face.

All of life rejoices that you are here,
an integral and crucial part of the whole,
separate yet connected
to nature's great mystery,
and blessed by one and all.

## CHILD OF EARTH AND SPACE

Child of Earth and space,
more than half of your body,
like this planet, is water.
Inside you, electricity, like lightning,
sparks and flares to its own rhythm.
You are trillions of tangible cells
yet your every atom
was created in the stars.

Child of Earth and space,
you are land and sky, water, and fire,
fed by the rich earth
yet born of distant galaxies.
The soil that nourishes you
is ancient mammals, birds, and insects,
eroded rocks, wood, and fossils.
You are nature's long and treasured stories;
a saga of miracles and magic.

Child of Earth and space,
you are storm clouds of electrons
governed by universal laws.
Entangled in nature's web,
you are an intimate part
of all creation.
You are life's tale in the telling,
evolution's latest chapter
and its newest song.

## OUR PROMISE TO YOU

Each one of us gathered here today
promises to protect you, *dear one*,
promises to love and nurture you,
to be tolerant and patient with you,
to respect and honour you,
to help and educate you;

to give up our precious time for you,
even when pressing matters call,
to offer you our full attention,
our advice, ideas, our all.

We will play and laugh with you,
and keep you safe from harm,
feeling grateful that we know you
and honoured by your presence,
for you are one of us
and one of the Whole.

## NAMING CEREMONY

We choose this name
to represent your spirit and fire,
and to signify your beauty and potential.
We offer this name
to portray your innate power and wisdom,
and to recognise your uniqueness and
distinction.
We present this name
to mark your place among others
and your right to walk upon the Earth.
We speak this name,
a symbol of who you are and the love you
represent.
And the name we choose is:

..................................

## TEDDY BEARS AND BOUQUETS

Teddy bears and bouquets marked your coming.
Neighbours called, with quiet voices and steps,
to glimpse your tiny head among the sheets.
Relatives gladly passed on hand-me-downs,
while Nana rejoiced in knitting you things.

At night when you woke, hungry and distraught,
you were cradled and rocked in careful arms,
as we sat on your great-grandmother's chair,
recalling ancestors of long ago
who had brought us finally to this point.

Later, when owls screeched and new lambs
bleated,
mimicking your cry, we dashed to your side,
scurrying barefoot through hallway darkness,
forever desperate to hold you tight
and gaze in wonder at what had arrived.

We considered your looks, disposition,
health and deep-rooted familial traits.
Yet one thing was certain: we would never
be able to predict or estimate
who you would be; you were your own person.

From the start, little newcomer, you were
beyond our comprehension and control;
weak and so vulnerable, yet wiser
than millennia, every cell programmed
by some great power to grow and become.

## BLESSING FOR AN INFANT

May health and strength be with you,
may gentleness be your friend,
may hope beat within your heart
and compassion never end.
May you feel joy and wonder,
inspiration and true love.
May our earnest hopes and prayers
rain down blessings from above.

## IMPACT

Little do any of us know the impact we will have on *this baby/child*. And, in turn, *he/she* will have an impact on us.

Remember that when we smile at someone, we brighten a day that could otherwise have been sad, dark, or solitary.

When we offer praise, we lift people up. They may recall our words for weeks or even years to come. Our words may inspire them to do great things.

When we make a joke or a humorous remark, we raise someone's spirits; we help them to feel a moment of joy.

When we listen to someone's troubles, without judgement or interruption, we help them to feel heard and recognised. We help them to make sense of the chaos and confusion in their lives.

When we suggest advice, and it's accepted, that advice may become part of someone's outlook or even their daily routine. Our experience becomes part of theirs.

When we offer our opinion, someone will consider our point of view, perhaps even adopting it into their own world view. Our ideas may become part of the wiring of their brain.

When we reach out a hand to the desperate and despairing, we offer hope and encouragement – possibly even the will to carry on. Our compassion can be life-saving.

So, never underestimate the impact you have on others. Never underestimate the effect others have on you.

Choose your words and actions wisely. Choose them always with love.

## THIS MOMENT

Somewhere, under a cloud festival,
a gazing infant lies;
a kingfisher embraces
a stream's quiet meander;
a man with a half-smile
feels the world beneath his feet;
a dew-eyed calf wonders.

While here, evening ambers
the chestnut canopy,
as it shares leaf-breath
with air from my lungs,
and electrons orbiting my every atom
know they are planets circling
this moment's sun.

## EARLY MORNING

Dew glistens the grey meadow. Light seeps
through cloud strata to silver the vale.
Treading the field in reverence, heads bowed,
silent heifers commence morning prayer.
Even swishing hooves are stifled
by the closeness of cloud, the stillness of air.

From somewhere, a rook scratches at sky –
its wings, snagged threads in silk –
till reluctant mist dissipates
and pine trees castellate the hill.

Now, like a tossed coin, night flips
and the vale is gilded with morning
and every tree bursts with blackbird and robin
singing the promise of dawn.

## BINDWEED

Mist hems us in.
Wetsuit-tight, the damp clings;
summer is on the turn.

But, hopeful, bright, and bold –
like you, little ones –
we find pristine bindweed
weaving between leaves,
ornamentally strewn
over faded saplings
like festive lights.

And between each shining bloom
sinuous tendrils twine,
tightly binding on to life,

as your radiant faces glow
and your tight fingers entwine mine.

You know the trust
we all must come to know;
you know the love that binds.

## CHAPTER 2
## COMING OF AGE AND LEAVING HOME

*"She made herself stronger by fighting with the wind."*
*– Frances Hodgson Burnett (The Secret Garden)*

## AS YOU STEP FORTH

As you step forth into the world,
beyond the safety of these walls,
beyond the warmth of our home,
beyond our embrace and protection,
the scent of the hearth
still clinging to your clothes,
home-cooked meals
still lingering on your tongue,
family words and mannerisms
now a part
of your skin and bones,
remember that
you carry us with you;
wherever you go, we go too –
as you will always be a part of us,
and we will be a part of you.

In your heart, you hold
our love, hopes, dreams, and pride,
our family line,
our visions, tales, and schemes.
Feel us there with you
in the spring of your hopeful step,
in the brightness of your smile,
in the love we have bestowed upon you
for you to give freely
to friends anew.

## DO NOT BE AFRAID

Do not be afraid but hold your head high.

Do not be afraid, but always follow your instincts.

Do not be afraid to use the wealth of knowledge you have gained.

Do not be afraid to seek the help of others, as everyone sometimes must do.

Do not be afraid but use caution when you must.

Do not be afraid but believe in your own worth and ability.

Do not be afraid to emit light and love on a world sorely in need.

Do not be afraid to shine.

**WHAT I WANT TO SAY TO YOU**

That you're perfect as you are.
That if people try to diminish you,
belittle you, reject you,
it's not a reflection of your own worth,
but an acknowledgement of their lack.

That a single glimmer in your eye
is enough to ignite a universe,
to power the dreams
of nations.

That you have always been worthy
exactly as you are.
That the world is waiting for you,
needs you, wants you –

not as you will be
in ten years' time,
or twenty,
or when you have knowledge,
confidence,
wisdom,
wealth...

but as you are now,
in this instant,
in all your perfect imperfection.

That the world will sometimes trip you up,
make you falter and fall,
but the power contained in a single cell
of your adored being
has the strength to conquer all.

Be brave, my beauty, be brave,
for the world, it awaits.

## TOUCH THE EARTH*

Remember, from time to time,
to touch the earth,
to feel the soft wet grass
beneath your feet,
to smell the honeysuckle,
wild garlic and meadowsweet.

Remember, from time to time,
to dance with the wind,
to turn up your face
and greet the rain,
to embrace winter's chill
and summer's stillness.

Remember, from time to time,
to rest your weary head
on mossy banks
in quiet meadow corners
beneath reaching boughs
of sycamore and oak.

Remember, from time to time,
wherever you may be,
that you're a child of nature,
a part of the whole,
inseparable, connected,
body, mind and soul.

And remember
that in nature
you're always home.

*"Touch the earth, love the earth, honour the earth, her plains, her valleys, her hills, and her seas; rest your spirit in her solitary places." — Henry Beston, 'The Outermost House: A Year of Life on the Great Beach of Cape Cod'

## TRAVELLING THROUGH STORMS

Dearest darling,
What you are enduring now is part of life's great
test.
It hurts, I know. It hurts.
But when you are older and recall this
tempestuous time,
you will smile (yes, smile!) and realise
this pain, fear, and sorrow
are just a tiny tug
in your full and contented heart.

So, relish all experience –
the joyful and the turbulent –
as it is forming you;
making you who you will become:
a complete person,
full of love and compassion.

Love requires that you care not only for others,
but for yourself – fully.
That you accept and respect yourself
so that you can treat others with the same
regard.

Faith requires that you become
the very best that you can be
in every circumstance:
a shining ray of hope
in a dark and raging sky.

So, be quiet when you must,
move slowly and with patience.
Breathe deeply and be still,
so that you may endure these stormy times,
emerging all the greater.

As a tree puts down roots
to hold itself firm against the blast,
you too are being strengthened.
A whole and rounded person is being moulded –
full of life, love, and wisdom –
a beacon of light
for others who travel through storms.

# THE GREAT UNDOING

It is said that we only come to know who we truly are by unlearning all we have been taught to be; by finding our own methods, views, and tastes.

By unpicking the stitches of life's well-worn clothes, we discover the fabric anew, see its potential, re-envision it, sewing it together in fresh and inventive ways, using creative stitches of our own design.

It is said that the careful unravelling of our old, habitual ways will bring about a new understanding, a coming to terms, even a flourishing.

And this great undoing will be our making.

So, unpick all your delicate stitches, select new patterns and materials, in quirky designs and vibrant shades.

Flaunt your multicoloured wonder, your unashamed uniqueness and rainbow style until you feel bold and unparalleled – the person you were meant to be, free and whole.

## AS YOU GO

Your stride is long,
your head always proud,
ears alert for secrets
in the swelling breeze,
rattling branches,
billowing cloud.

Your long hair rivers,
catching eddies
of drifting tides,
which wrap around
your shoulders
like a cloak of sighs.

Your loping gait –
deceptively swift –
takes heed of Earth's
springtime vow:
new life and longing
beneath quick-stepping feet.

And young roots
in the deep pit of becoming
twine and curl,
urging you on,
you child of the universe,
you part of the One.

## A BLESSING AS YOU LEAVE

May you have food on the table,
a warm, comfortable home,
may love always travel with you
wherever you roam.

May you have health and happiness,
the company of friends,
and may Spirit be beside you
at long journey's end.

## UNFOLDING LIKE LILIES
*(Chester)*


March's blast assaults us.
Mugger-gusts knife through alleys.
Toiling up Frodsham Street, they thrash us
then hurtle, remorseless,
over rooftops, braced
and clinging.

Storm-blown ships, we pitch on the Eastgate
Rows,
where timbers groan in momentary lulls.
People group, conspiratorial,
in penguin huddles by the city wall,
or loiter in synthetic precinct
to creep out stiff as spiders.

Reminding us to be gracious,
the woolly capped faithful
stand buffeted beneath Bridge Street Cross,
handing out hot cross buns
to the reluctant grateful,
who snatch, nod, hurry off.

In Northgate Square, we are spun
in a cyclone of leaves.
So we plunge
into cathedral shadow
to find ourselves held
in rare and sudden stillness.

Entering the nave, we sigh,
unfolding like lilies on gentle water,
blossoming into
a pool of peace –
that quiet distillation
of centuries of prayer.

## SYMPHONY

I shall inhale you.

I shall snatch you from the air
and breathe you in,
you shining minims, crotchets,
whirling semi-quavers.
And you'll tinkle like bells
through the hairs of my nose,
tingling, tingling.

Prestissimo violins,
you'll scurry down my throat,
flurry to fill
the great hall of my lungs,
where alveoli are choristers
and hallelujahs echo
under my ribcage dome.
You'll sing and sing.

From here, I shall absorb you.
Tumbling kettle-drums,
you'll bubble-burst
into the thunder
of my blood,
where you'll gush to the rhythm
of my timpani heart,
pounding, pounding.

You will stir
my very core
with your frantic dancing.
You will orchestrate my song.
And the music I breathe
shall be joy.

## CHAPTER 3
## HANDFASTING AND MARRIAGE

*"But let there be spaces in your togetherness*
*and let the winds of the heavens dance*
*between you.*
*Love one another but make not a bond of love:*
*let it rather be a moving sea*
*between the shores of your souls."*
*– Khalil Gibran ('On Marriage')*

## LOVE IS THE HIGHEST FORM OF BEING

*('handfasting' can be changed to 'marriage / wedding/ blessing' as appropriate)*

................ and ............... know that their meeting was meant to be. The universe, in its astonishing synchronicity, has brought them together, and today is a celebration of the profound and heartfelt trust that has developed between them – a trust that will continue to be nurtured during their lives.

Two people, who were alone and apart, have come together to form a completeness, a sense of solidarity, a mutual understanding. Their lives have been made fuller.

In this *handfasting*, as we celebrate their deep love for one another, we recognise that love is the highest form of being. Love is the core of the universe. Love is at the heart of all worthwhile human endeavours. Love is the central theme of all religions and beliefs. All deeds performed in the name of love are therefore holy and blessed.

This *handfasting* is performed in the name of love.

We acknowledge the love that ............... and ............... have for one another. We acknowledge the love that this congregation has for this couple and for each other. We acknowledge that love exists here and now in this special place.

## MAKING PROMISES

My friend, my love, _my partner_,
I promise to love, cherish, and respect you
as my equal,
to appreciate each day spent with you,
and to never take you for granted.

I promise to be tolerant and patient,
kind and understanding
when fatigue, ill health, or stressful times
challenge us and wear us down,
knowing that we are stronger together.

I promise to work hard,
to evolve as a human being,
to give something back to the world,
but also to rest when I need to
so our lives maintain balance.

I promise to walk beside you
on your journey,
comforting and supporting you
when you are weary, downcast
or in despair.

I promise to celebrate your achievements,
to acknowledge them with pride,
feeling jubilation and triumph for you
as if your accomplishments
were my own.

And I promise that when energy lessens
and bones and muscles ache
and old age whispers from around the corner,
when romance turns naturally to friendship,
I will not seek the arms of another.

I will not give up on you
for you are my most trusted companion;
I will thank you for all you have given me
and I will praise you
for all you have done.

My soul mate, my love, _my partner_,
through these promises
we create together
a future of promise.

## WHAT IS A PARTNERSHIP?

It is not putting down; it is building up.

It is not taking for granted; it is noticing.

It is not envying; it is celebrating.

It is not assuming; it is listening.

It is not demanding; it is appreciating.

It is not judging; it is trying to understand.

It is not condemning; it is forgiving.

It is not controlling; it is setting free.

It is loving and loving … and loving.

## THESE TWO HANDS

As these two hands are twined,
so are your hearts.

As these two hands are twined,
so are your minds.

As these two hands are twined,
so are your bodies.

As these two hands are twined,
so are your souls.

As your hands come together
so do your lives,
bound by a common cause:
to love, support and nurture,
to encourage and inspire
each other to become
the best that you can be.

Two souls, united as one,
your sole purpose:
love.

## RINGS

Circles of glinting light –
bright unbreakable bands –
symbolising the strength
of joining your two hands.

Circles of glinting light –
a never-ending line –
representing your love
continuing for all time.

## THIS POEM IS A BLESSING
*('handfasting' can be changed to*
*'marriage/wedding/blessing' as appropriate)*

This poem is a blessing;
it will travel with you
wherever you go.

It will not end
when doors close,
when lights dim,
when pathways stop,
when the day is done.

It will continue with you,
like a loyal friend,
across roiling seas,
on new and steep tracks
and jagged mountain paths.

There is no limit to its distance,
no restriction on its depth,
no failing in its intent;
it neither fades nor ceases.

And you will feel it again
in the warmth of hearths,
in a glimpse of bright stars,
in the comforting words
of strangers.

And you will be reminded
of this time, this place,
this precious _handfasting_,
of encouragement and support
gathering, forming, growing
into a blessing of such magnitude,
it is eternal and mighty:
a blessing of unbreakable love.

## LOVE IS*

If I speak the language of saints and mystics
but I do not feel love rising
in my soul,
then my words will be hollow.

If I can predict the future,
understanding the realms of science and spirit,
but I do not predict with love,
then my prophecy will have no purpose.

If I believe, with all my heart,
in the power of prayer and intent,
but love is absent from my thoughts,
then my intercessions will have no point.

If I give away all my belongings,
sell my possessions to feed the poor,
but do this for ego and not for love,
then my gifts will be worthless.

Love is kindness, honesty, optimism,
acceptance, tolerance, compassion.
It never angers, scolds, or lashes out.

Love is brave, humble, calm, forgiving.
Full of integrity, it is selfless and fair.
It never resorts to pride, conceit or envy.

Love is hope.
Love is trust.
True love endures all.

*Inspired by Corinthians 1:13 (The Bible)*

## MR. & MRS. ARNOLD

This is a true story. Back in the summer of 2021, in a wildlife centre in New England, an unexpected visitor had arrived without an appointment. Worse still, seemingly agitated, she was knocking rudely on the window. Somehow, she had tracked down her injured partner (recently named Arnold) who was undergoing surgery. Arnold was a Canada goose.

Single-mindedly and risking all, she had waddled from their nearby pond up to the building. She had even located the correct window! Now, insistently tapping with her beak, she was demanding entry.

Undeterred by the many astonished gazes, Mrs. Arnold settled in on the porch and peered through the glass door with her beady eyes, focusing solely on her mate, whose broken foot was being treated. Of course, Arnold, floppy-necked and anaesthetised, was not looking at his best. But she didn't seem to mind.

Gradually, Arnold came round and, with his lower lids, opened his bleary eyes. Wrapped in a warm blanket, he was carried carefully to the glass door, which was opened slightly so that Mrs. Arnold could reach inside.

Preening him gently, she stayed beside him "in sickness and in health." She was fearless and wholehearted in her commitment. And, instantly, they both seemed calmer, more reassured, and quite obviously besotted.

And isn't that what we all want from a partner?

Someone who will go out of their way for us.

Someone who will take chances for us.

Someone who doesn't care what anyone else thinks.

Someone who will be with us fearlessly and completely.

After all, for Mrs. Arnold there was no alternative and no doubt: Canada geese mate for life.

## MARRIAGE BLESSING*

Now you will feel no sorrow
as you will be gladness for each other.
Now you will feel no pain
as you will be healing for each other.
Now you will feel no loneliness
as you will be companionship for each other.
Now you will feel no harshness
as you will be tenderness for each other.
Now you will feel no greed
as you will be abundance for each other.

Now you will understand
that the Creator has brought you together;
that Mother Earth and Father Sky
bless you from below and above;
that you will take only what you need
from nature's great bounty;
that you will guide each other
in caring for creation's beauty;
that you will guide each other
in expressing your abundant love.

*Inspired by an Apache blessing from North America*

## A POET'S LOVES
*(For Andrew)*


Not only is it language she loves –
words, set free, skittle-tumbling down the page,
shades of meaning tapestry-weaving
their intricate colour-play.

Not only is it sound she treasures –
echoing half-rhymes and verse
washing like breakers on shingle shores;
the soothing of her universe.

Not only is it subtlety she craves –
pausing, alluding, choosing words
to be unsaid, or phrases like autumn roses
pruned hard back.

It's how he tries to classify her scribble-scratch
ideas;
how he ponders her, reads her like a book;
how, snug as pages, he holds her near;
how always he fears her final full stop.

# CHAPTER 4
# MISCARRIAGE AND THE DEATH OF A CHILD

*"She burned too bright for this world."*
*– Emily Brontë (Wuthering Heights)*

## THE EARTH SIGHS

The Earth sighs collectively.
Then silence – numb and
uncomprehending.

A holding of breath
as minds try to digest
this painful new reality:

a hollowness, an emptiness
where once there was hope,
potential, life.

A space never to be refilled
exists in the world,
like an abandoned home
or unrequited love.

Birds, formerly vocal,
singing of territories,
mates, and young,
fall still.

Sheep in the fields
hit the ground heavily,
hunkering down,
as if waiting for night to pass.

Clouds sail overhead,
marking time and space,
though we are not part of it.

And all the while
our heads spin,
our hearts ache,
tears well...

This new reality
is not something
we were consulted on.

At no point
did we ever agree
to losing you.

## LULLABY

Sleep, my baby,
shut your eyes;
angels call you
from on high.

Rest in peace now,
don't you wake;
lie so still while
our hearts break.

Though apart now,
you'll remain
in our spirit,
where you'll stay.

Tiny breaths and
tiny sighs;
your voice whispers
from the sky.

Slumber deeply,
with the One;
shine so brightly
with the sun.

Sleep, my baby,
rest your head;
angels rock you
in my stead.

While you're dreaming
wait for me;
soon I'll hold you
eternally.

## COME GENTLY
*(Use 'him/her/them/their name' and 'little one/dearest one' in this prayer as appropriate)*

Come gently,
winds of the north, south, east, and west,
bringing soft, healing rains,
come to take our *little one* home.

Come gently,
gliding birds of the air
and creatures of this precious Earth,
come to take our *little one* home.

Come gently,
beloved ancestors who have gone before us,
over many generations and in many lands,
come to take our *little one* home.

Rock *her* gently in your tender arms.
Hold *her* close to your love-filled hearts.
Carry *her* back towards the light;
carry our *little one* home.

## BABY

A baby – firm in our minds,
but foetus-flimsy in the womb.
We wanted you, loved you,
hoped for you;
now we must return you,
your short life complete.

## PRAYER OF MOURNING
*(Use 'he/she/they' and 'him/her/them' in this prayer as appropriate)*


Dear Sacred Spirit,
Our hearts are aching
and we can hardly bear the loss.
Please call upon your shining angels,
those beings of perfect light,
to greet our *little one*
as *she* comes to you now.

Wrap your gentle arms around *her*
and draw *her* close.
Surround *her* with protective light
and warming, soothing love.
Prepare a place for *her*
in the many-roomed house
of your ever-caring realm.

Let *her* sleep peacefully there,
feeling safe and nurtured,
until one day, when we hear your gentle call,
we will come to find *her,*
to be united with *her.*
We will all come back home.

## THANK YOU

Thank you for coming into our lives – if only for a short while.

Thank you for reminding us of the preciousness of life and the delicacy of nature.

Thank you for teaching us that life often hangs in the balance – sacred and fragile.

Thank you for making us see that each day is a gift – which not everyone will receive.

Thank you for inspiring us to live each moment that is given to us, gratefully.

Thank you for blessing us with your dear and treasured presence.

## RIVERS BREAK THEIR BANKS

Such a length of night. Lying still,
I hold my breath and listen.
Rain kettle-drums the gutters,
wind-whipping trees roar.
I sound the darkest reaches
to locate the clock's tick –
sure and heartbeat-steady.
I part folds of blackness
to find my husband's slumber;
his breath touches me
from immeasurable night.

My own breathing startles me;
its reflex audacity.
Listening again, at sound's margin,
is the subtle groan of flesh –
my belly's bloatedness;
a shocking emptiness where once
a small being floated,
pistoned new-found feet,
tasted sprouted fingers, wriggled
for the joy of it and slept.

Outside, the storm rages,
snapping ancient oaks.
And rivers break their banks:
a turmoil of clay-red waters
rush into flood plains to swamp
a softness of gentle land.

## OYSTER CATCHER

As the tide withdrew
and my feet explored damp, soft sand,
I found oyster catcher tracks
meandering near the surf.

Three outstretched claws,
with one behind, looked like
budding flowers or the peace sign
let loose upon the beach.

But soon they stopped,
vanishing without trace.
I pondered their disappearance;
felt a kind of loss.

Then I realised
what must have occurred;
peered heavenwards
to shining sky and gliding cloud.

Like you, *my dearest darling*,
the bird no longer walked on land;
it sailed above my head,
its strong wings outstretched,

feeling the breeze in its feathers,
warm sunlight on its back,
playing with dancing eddies,
elated and free at last.

## A GENTLE CHASM

My husband breathes
in a womb of sleep; the clock ticks,
but time halts, draws breath
like a gift-opening child.

I notice stillness, silence,
something like light.
A gentle chasm tears the night,
leaves it gaping, waiting...

Someone is here, yet
less than a fissure
shows the space you fill
and you take no space at all.

Awake as a dawn cockerel,
I peer into haze. Dark
is alive; it flickers
fainter than fireside brasses
or far-sparking heather
on our Clwydian Hills.
And, somehow, I know it's you,
and I know you're more alive than I.

Next day, approaching the farm,
I pause, recall a quiet joy,
a half-held dream, then join
your trembling family, tears
spilling over like exploding bombs
or fresh-cut lilies, dripping.

## SWEET AIR

The very first sweep of swallows
skims then soars, breezing
my hair. April high jinks –
just back from Africa.
Their electric joy
sweetening the air;
edging in.

Embossed on cloudless blue,
a spire-top blackbird sings,
while cool dusk stretches
your gravestone shadow
across bowed narcissi,
keeping vigil.

And I feel
sweet air
softly, kindly
seeping in.

# CHAPTER 5
# CELEBRATING CHILDREN AND BIRTHDAYS


*"It is more fun to talk with someone who doesn't use long, difficult words*
*but rather short easy words like 'What about lunch?'"*
*– A. A. Milne (Winnie the Pooh)*

**PRAYER**\*

Dear Great Spirit of Life,
You are everywhere
and we love you.

We are listening to hear your voice
and to find your wisdom
in the lessons of nature
and the company of friends,
so that we can play our part
in making the sad happy,
the polluted clean
and the future hopeful.

Thank you for every day and every minute.
Help us to be patient with ourselves when we
make mistakes
and help us to forgive others when they upset
us.

Fill us with your energy and inspire us to be
brave and kind.
The universe is huge and mighty;
it goes on forever.
But the heart of everything
is love.

*\*Inspired by The Lord's Prayer*

## TREE MEDITATION
*(A grounding practice for children)*


Stretch up your arms. Higher! Higher!
Plant your feet firmly on the ground.
Now, imagine you're a tree;
your arms are long branches, and your fingers
are tiny twigs.
Reach up, reach up!
You're tall and impressive, ancient and mighty.

What sort of tree will you be?
An oak, a beech, an ash?
Maybe a palm tree, or a giant red wood
towering above the forest?

My goodness, I can see something!
What do you have sitting on your branches?
What are you sheltering in your leafy canopy?
Pigeons, crows, woodpeckers? Robins perhaps?
Do squirrels scratch your bark as they scamper
about?
What about foxes and badgers sniffing around
your roots?
Does their breath tickle?

Now, lower your arms and take a deep breath.
As you breathc out, allow your hands to flop
down, and close your eyes gently.
Imagine, imagine ...

Roots are growing down your backbone,
down through your legs and into your feet.
They're reaching and reaching,
bursting out of your body and into the soil.
Your roots are fast and powerful;
they move quickly through mud, water, sand,
and stones.

Can you feel the layers of earth beneath you?
Your roots are so strong that
when gales blow your branches wildly about,
making your trunk sway and bend,
you never fall over.
You're anchored safely in the ground.

Can you feel a great storm coming?
Hold tight!

Now, as the wind dies down,
keep very still;
concentrate on your feet.
The ground below you is full of tingly energy;
it rises up from the great fire at the centre of the
Earth.

Feel it climbing up through your roots
and into your sturdy trunk,
up through your branches and into your leaves.
It makes you feel warm and safe and loved.

As you feel this tingly power
flooding your body and creeping upwards,
you can also feel something warm and bright

on the top of your head.
It's the sun's rays shining on your canopy;
it feels delightful.

The sunlight glints on your green leaves;
it warms your small twigs and strong boughs.
You feel loved from the sky above
and loved from the tingly ground.

Take a deep breath then release it slowly.
Enjoy being a beautiful, strong tree
standing in the sunshine.
Notice the blue sky overhead,
the breeze whispering in your leaves,
the little animals sheltering in your branches,
the sunlight warming you from above
and the Earth's energy warming you from
below...

And, when you're ready, open your eyes and say,
"Thank you, dear Earth.
Thank you, dear Sun."

## BLESSING FOR A CHILD

May your friends always be true,

may family be at your side,

may light shine down upon you

and nature soothe your mind.

May daytime bring you laughter

and night-time deepest peace,

may dreams become your guiding stars,

may wonder never cease.

## THE UNIVERSE IS IN CONTROL

*(A meditation practice for children – this may help with sleeping problems or anxiety if they're feeling restless or worried)*

Lie down on the bed (*or floor*) and make yourself comfortable.

Take a deep breath and let it go – slowly.
Feel your body sinking into the mattress (*or floor*).

Take another deep breath and let it go.
Now, close your eyes gently and listen to my voice ...

First of all, turn your toes up towards you, as far as you can, so you feel a big stretch up the back of your legs.

Hold it for a few seconds. And relax.

Next, squeeze your knees tightly, so you feel your legs tightening up.
Notice your strong thigh muscles clenching.
Hold it and then let go. Good.

Now, tighten your stomach; make it feel like a knot.
Notice your belly button moving back towards your spine.
Hold it ... and release.

67

Make your hands into fists and squeeze them
hard.
Stay like this for a few seconds and then let go.
Straighten your arms until they feel like stiff
planks of wood;
make all your muscles clench, and then relax.
Now, press down your shoulders; pull them
down away from your neck.
Hold them, and release. Good.

Lastly, scrunch up your eyes tightly, and then
relax them –
but keep them closed.

Feel your whole body relax.
Every muscle is soft, and every bone is heavy.
You're sinking deeper and deeper into the
mattress (*or floor*).

Down, down, down you go ...
As you sink down, I want you to use your
imagination.
Listen carefully to my voice and imagine what I
say.

You're lying in a little wooden rowing boat and
you're floating out to sea.

You're exactly where you should be, and you're
completely safe.

You feel very comfortable, bobbing up and down
on the gentle waves.

68

It's a warm night and the stars are shining in the velvety black sky.

The salty smell of the sea makes your nostrils tingle.

You can feel a soft breeze drifting over your body and through your hair.

Breathe slowly and enjoy how it feels.
You're drifting further and further out to sea now,
but you feel calm, cosy, peaceful, and safe.

Now, even though you hadn't noticed it,
the rowing boat is floating gently into the air.
It's rising off the water and sailing higher and higher.
The little boat is carrying you up into the sky.

You feel tired, warm, and dreamy,
so you just lie there and enjoy the ride.
And soon you're floating among the twinkling stars,
sailing through the deep black night,
and you don't mind where you go
or how long it takes you.

The universe is in control, not you.
It's guiding you on your journey
and you're going in just the right direction
all the time.

You don't have to worry about a thing.
You feel comfortable and sleepy.

You know you're safe and you know you're loved.
It's a wonderful feeling.

You're in harmony with everything,
a part of the big plan,
as important as the planets,
as important as the stars.

And while you're sailing through deep, deep
space,
the universe smiles on you,
and you know you're loved
and you know you're safe.

*(If you want your child to go to sleep, stop here!
Otherwise carry on...)*

And when you've enjoyed the velvety darkness
and sparkling stars,
and you feel it's time to sail back home,
the little rowing boat drifts back down towards
your house.

It floats in through the open window
and places you softly in your bed *(or on the floor)*.

And when you feel ready to open your eyes,
you will know for certain
that you're an important part of everything,

that you can relax and smile
because the universe has a plan for you;
the universe is in control.

## RAP FOR THE PLANET

I'm a child, not an adult,
but I know what I feel:
I'm a part of the universe
and it's a part of me.
I'm not just bones and muscles,
a beating heart and brain;
I'm a wild child of nature.
Don't you feel the same?
The moon pulls the oceans;
the wind moves the clouds.
Don't you feel involved in it?
Shout 'yes' clear and loud!
Everything's connected,
including you and me;
we're made of distant stardust,
saltwater in the sea.
Birds fly with the seasons,
leaves fall from the trees,
flowers burst from darkness
saved by tiny honey bees.
This planet is amazing;
it gives us air to breathe,
cool water when we're thirsty,
and leaves and fruit to eat.
Let's save the Earth together;
the world is our best friend.
Respect the whole of nature
for on it we depend.

## HAPPY BIRTHDAY REMAKE

Happy birthday to you.
We love you – yes, we do!
May good luck go with you
and shenanigans too.

## THE BIRTHDAY MARCH
*(with apologies to Noah!)*


The animals marched in two by two.
Hurrah, hurrah!

The animals marched in two by two.
Hurrah, hurrah!

The animals marched in two by two –
the bear wanted to march with you –
and they all came marching
into the house for tea.

The animals marched in three by three.
Hurrah, hurrah!

The animals marched in three by three.
Hurrah, hurrah!

The animals marched in three by three –
the penguin, fox, and chimpanzee –
and they all came marching
into the house for tea.

The animals marched in four by four.
Hurrah, hurrah!

The animals marched in four by four.
Hurrah, hurrah!

The animals marched in four by four –
someone had to widen the door –
and they all came marching
into the house for tea.

The animals marched in five by five.
Hurrah, hurrah!

The animals marched in five by five.
Hurrah, hurrah!

The animals marched in five by five –
Grandmother shouted, "Snakes alive!" –
and they all came marching
into the house for tea.

The animals marched in six by six.
Hurrah, hurrah!

The animals marched in six by six.
Hurrah, hurrah!

The animals marched in six by six –
the rabbits did some magic tricks –
and they all came marching
into the house for tea.

The animals marched in droves and herds.
Hurrah, hurrah!

The animals marched in droves and herds.
Hurrah, hurrah!

The animals marched in droves and herds –
the spotted, striped, feathered, and furred –
and they all came marching
into the house for tea...

until Mum said,
"Oi! What are you lot doing here?
It's _Billy's_ party, not yours! Clear off!"
So they all traipsed out.

THE END

P.S. You should have seen the mess.
P.P.S. I persuaded Mum to let us keep the bear.

## DINAS BRAN, LLANGOLLEN

We clambered the hill's crumbling skin –
children and dogs scattering,
teetering goat-like on rims –
our breath and legs burning,
laughter snatched by the wind.

Halfway to the crown,
a tapestry stilled us – tree-and-river stitches
fading into Cheshire haze –
while dogs and children leapt upon
the darting backs of ravens.

Spiders spinning webs of story,
we scaled the slope, linked
by threads of long ago,
as bright clouds skimmed like yesterdays
over a crumbling city of crows.

## JOE

Head down, gripping the pencil,
he copied marks she had made.
Sitting back, he studied them. How
could three letters of straight lines and curves
make Joe? How could they contain
Joe the explorer, Joe the artist, daring acrobat,
sometimes dog, cavorting on all fours,
and expert on dinosaurs? Why
should silly squiggle-shapes show
grasshopper dancing, impulsive
stillness, the joy that is Joe?
This writing's not all it's cracked up to be.
It's someone playing games, or cheating.
It's no mirror-image or rippling reflection;
it's simply the shadow of Joe,
in disguise and in the distance.

**FIRST SNOW**

You go rushing out: something about
"snow being pink"? Then I see you –
fingers wide, reaching
for falling, whirling blossom.
Petals mingle with dappled light,
flutter gentle as a festival.
And you, my crazy wind-up frog,
leap and pounce, and shriek.

At night, we hear the wind
hurling darkness between rafters,
sucking it out through gaps,
and lashing branches tap
drum rolls on the cracking slates.

Throwing back morning-bright curtains,
I see you – frowning, empty-palmed –
beneath the naked tree.
But pink velvet drifts
cushion the garden and clothe
your soft-kicking feet. And soon
petal-fountains spray like fireworks
about you, as you make the new day
another celebration.

## CHAPTER 6
## MIDDLE AGE AND GAINING WISDOM


*"Till this moment I never knew myself."*
*– Jane Austen (Pride and Prejudice)*

## MYSTERIES, MIRACLES, GIFTS

The universe is a mystery, a miracle, a gift.
We affirm that every planet, moon, and star –
including the Earth, our Moon and Sun – are
sacred in their unfathomable wonder.

The elements are a mystery, a miracle, a gift.
We acknowledge that all the components of life –
earth, water, fire, and air – are sacred and
fantastic in their complexity.

All of nature is a mystery, a miracle, a gift.
We celebrate that wherever we go – crossing
mountains, seas, deserts, and plains – nature is
sacred in its manifold landscapes.

All forms of life are a mystery, a miracle, a gift.
We give thanks that we share this planet with
others – flowers, trees, fish, mammals, insects,
reptiles, and more – who have the same history
of evolution, the same sacred source.

All people are a mystery, a miracle, a gift.
We feel blessed that we can befriend others – no
matter what their age, health, creed, or
experience – for they are all sacred, wise, and
radiant.

All knowledge is a mystery, a miracle, a gift.
We recognise that in whatever way we learn –
through study, observation, or experimentation –
knowledge is sacred in its multifarious modes.

All of us are a mystery, a miracle, a gift to one
another.
We give thanks for like-minded people, well-
travelled friends, and old souls.

## "WISDOM MAKES LIGHT THE DARKNESS OF IGNORANCE" *

"Wisdom makes light
the darkness of ignorance."

Knowledge makes clear
the cloudiness of unknowing.

Courage makes pure
the stagnation of cowardice.

Perseverance makes hopeful
the gloom of defeat.

Empathy makes whole
the brokenness of indifference.

Truth makes bright
the shadow of deceit.

Love makes warm
the iciness of hate.

And you, *dear one*, stand for all of these:
wisdom, knowledge, courage, perseverance,
empathy, truth, and love.

We acknowledge your understanding,
we respect your integrity,

we celebrate your light,
we love you for who you are.

*A quotation from Gautama Buddha*

## COMFORTABLE AT LAST

Comfortable at last in your own skin,
accepting of yourself
and tolerant of others.

Forgiving others' hurtfulness,
but not being taken
for a fool.

Saying it how it is –
but thoughtfully,
kindly.

Confident in your skills,
talents, and knowledge,
but keen to learn more.
Knowing your own weaknesses,
faults, and peculiarities
yet being patient with yourself.

Listening without speaking,
if that's what's needed,
and feeling at ease in the silence.

Pleased by the small things –
raindrops on windows,
friendships, and candlelight,
the first hot drink of the day,
well-fitting shoes.

Finding amusement
in your own mistakes
and humour
in your quirky ways.

Dancing in the kitchen,
singing in the car –
and not caring
what others think.

Forgiving yourself,
loving yourself,
encouraging yourself …

Welcome to middle age!
Welcome to wisdom!

## EARTH, TEACH ME*

Earth, teach me resilience
as a tall larch withstands a storm.

Earth, teach me bravery
as a gull defends its nest.

Earth, teach me respect
as a cub reveres the vixen.

Earth, teach me humility
as the river is humbled by the sea.

Earth, teach me selflessness
as the swallow feeds its fledglings.

Earth, teach me to begin again
as the cherry blossoms in spring.

Earth, teach me to remember
our many ancestors
who have walked this land before us,
teaching us wisely of love and respect

for all living things
and for ourselves.

Earth, teach me.

*Inspired by a prayer of the Ute people of North America*

## THE REALM OF SPIRIT

The realm of spirit is eternal;
it is everywhere and forever.
It is greater than any person,
city, land, or continent.
It is wiser and richer
than any book, law, or creed.
We all give something
to the realm of spirit.
No one is ever omitted
or excluded.
No one is ever unworthy
or forgotten.
Spirit is omnipresent,
in our cells and in our galaxies,
inseparable from the physical,
intertwined and complete.
There are many ways
to commune with spirit;
no one path is correct,
no one prayer is right,
no ceremony or service
is better than another.
We live in spirit right now;
new life and old
rejoice in this knowledge,
sharing in this unconditional love.
Find your own way
to connect with spirit;
find your own way
to everlasting peace and light.

**REIKI***

Just for today,
clouds will not darken
my valley of tranquillity;
no gales will stir whirlpools
in my sea of stillness.
My heart will paint
bright rainbows
across a vast sky
of abundance.

At work,
I will compose songs
at the top of my lungs,
like dawn birds giving their all.
And every living soul will feel
the radiance of my sunshine.
Just for today.

*Inspired by the Reiki Principles*

## ODE TO THE COSMOS

If I could reach out
and touch the hem
of your dark cloak
and gaze in wonder
at its sequined constellations,
its gold-stitched galaxies;
then I would know –
I would know the mystery of your depths.

If I could bask
in the shafts
of a single fiery star
embroidered on your mantle
and absorb its brilliance
without ever being scorched;
then I would know –
I would know the radiance of your light.

If I could raise,
for a moment,
the heavy cowl that
obscures your face and peer
into those fierce
yet forgiving eyes;
I would know –
I would know the power of your knowing.

And I would realise
that this yearning, burning,
smouldering in my heart,
which longs to reach out
far and beyond, can enfold
everyone and can hold
everyone in its glow –
though a mere flicker,
a scintilla of a spark,
beside your glorious blaze of love.

## GOING WITHIN

When the world presses in on me
and I cannot imagine
a future of worth
for myself and my family,
friends and community,
I breathe slowly and go within.

When great winds howl,
lifting slates and toppling trees,
and I cannot predict
a time of security
for the planet or me,
I breathe slowly and go within.

When people fall out
and harsh words are hurled
in anger and haste,
and I cannot discern
a way out of this hate,
I breathe slowly and go within.

When life is brimming
with pain and suffering,
when poverty reigns
and hunger is rife,
when I cannot find the answers required,
I breathe slowly and go inside.

And deep within,
where my heart beats softly
and my lungs do nothing
but breathe the air,
I know peace for a time
and my thoughts become quiet.

Then my mind casts off
and drifts through space,
sailing in silence
on vast waves of love,
part of one consciousness,
peaceful, cherished, and safe.

## IMPRESSIONS

It's one of those Monet days –
bursting brightness, dark dabs of shade;
the trees, a kinetic filigree
where insects on a dappled canvas
leave darts of memory.

But if you try less hard, give up
the scrutiny, for a time step back,
each straining grass is lost
in the grand dance of meadow,
every spiking bramble
is a stroke of hedgerow shadow,
an embrace for crumbling fence

and the whole picture seems clearer;
it seems to make sense.

## IF DEATH COMES
*(For Will and Ana)*


If death comes, but no chance has arisen
to hug you once more, to kiss you and smile,
you must understand that I am ready,
for I have enjoyed a beautiful life.

On spring days, I have sat, among cedars
and daffodils, with dear friends sipping tea;
I have walked Roman paths, bejewelled with
light,
between primrose and wood anemone.

In the bright haze of summer, I have swum
in cold Anglesey seas, quite mesmerised
by views of the distant Llŷn, calling gulls
and the magnetism of rolling tides.

During the wild, swirling winds of autumn,
I have stood on the Clwydian Hills,
close to Offa's Dyke, with my arms outstretched,
defying racing air, alive and thrilled.

In the chill of winter, gathering sticks
from under thick hedges, I have trudged home
through powdery snow and red setting sun
to the warm welcome of a burning stove.

I have wondered at creation's flora
and fauna: brother blackbird, sister fox.
I have been drenched in green-woodland
birdsong,
and trusted by various cats and dogs.

Dwarfed by the ancient Snowdonia peaks
or cloaked in a star-strewn, infinite sky,
I have felt minute, inconsequential,
yet inseparable from great majesty.

My greatest pride; my son and my daughter,
will continue exploring hills and shores,
knowing that I was both loved and loving;
who of us could ask for anything more?

# CHAPTER 7
## FUNERALS AND MOURNING

*"Faith is the bird that feels the light
when the dawn is still dark."
– Rabindranath Tagore*

## DREAMING AND WAKING

As you slip in and out of sleep,
a new possibility calls you.
As sense of place becomes confused,
a new location draws you.
As dreaming and waking blur,
a greater dream beguiles you.

It occupies you more and more,
this dream of continuing self.
Like a far-off vision,
it enthrals you,
until dreaming becomes waking,
though you wake somewhere else.

## LETTING GO


As we let go of you, of your love, care, and
warmth,
your thoughts, humour, and ideas,
we know that you, too, have had to let go –
of your ambitions, dreams, and plans,
the ones you achieved, and the ones left
unfulfilled.

So, we breathe and let you go.

As we let go of you, of your life, home, and
treasures,
your prized possessions
and scattered trinkets,
we know that you, too, have had to let go –
of favourite drinks and tasty meals,
of clothes, books, ornaments, and art.

So, we breathe and let you go.

As we let go of you, of your smile, touch, and
embrace,
the way you comforted us and held us,
your wise words and kind advice,
we know that you, too, have had to let go –
of friendships, loves, and companions,
of the soft touch of another's hand.

So, we breathe and let you go.

And as we release you into the universe,
its stars, rivers, hills, and seas,
its winds, sunshine, and winter frost,
we know that you have known the ultimate
release –
letting go of colours, smells, seasons,
the light of day and the dark of night,
the setting sun and rising moon.

So, we breathe and let you go,
returning you to All That Is,
allowing you
to find your way home.

## A PRAYER OF BESEECHING
*(Use 'he/she/they' and 'him/her/them' in this prayer as appropriate)*

Dear Sacred Spirit,
We beseech you,
as our hearts are breaking
and we can hardly bear the loss,
to call upon the angels of the higher realms,
those beings of perfect light,
the holy and revered,
and our loved ones long since gone.
Gather them together,
in their wondrous glory,
to greet dear ..........................
as *he* comes to you now.

Wrap your tender arms around *him*
and draw *him* close.
Surround *him* with protective light
and warming, soothing love.
Prepare a place for *him*
in the many-roomed house
of your ever-caring realm.
Let *him* know you love *him*
as much as we do,
as much as it is possible to love.

Allow *him* to be at peace there,
to feel safe and nurtured,
joyful and liberated,

until one day, when we hear your gentle call,
we will come to find *him*,
to be reunited with *him*.
We will all come back home.

## IN THE DARK GREEN PLACES

In the dark green places
of the woods,
where light barely seeps through,
among the creeping lichens
and soft-pillowed moss,
we will find you.

In the heavy cloak of night,
among fiery stars
and shooting meteors,
where owls hoot
and bats outwit the dark,
we will remember you.

In the bright sunny days
of wind and surf,
where light bounces off
the rippling sea
and gulls cry from azure skies,
we will thank you.

In the ventricles
of our beating hearts,
as our blood pumps
through veins and arteries,
determined and ongoing,
we will know you.

And we will feel you
as close as blood,
as endless as nebulae.

## AS MOTHER NATURE DECREES

As Mother Nature decrees, all new growth must come from dying. We see it in the growing of tiny seeds in soil's rich decay. And we see it in the cycle of the seasons: the sprouting of spring shoots and the blossoming of flowers after the bleakness and desolation of winter. When we feel that all hope is gone, when the days are short and harsh, and the nights long and bitter, we finally sense regeneration – a stirring of something vital in the air and ground. And brave snowdrops rear their dainty heads, showing us for certain that life's endurance is profound.

As it is in nature, so it is in our lives: our first steps, our first words are the snowdrops of January and the primroses of spring. When summer comes, we have bloomed and grown tall, beautiful, and fragrant. We are in our prime! Our midlife is the autumn, when we sense the creeping frosts of winter ahead, when we conserve energy and bloom our last. Winter is a quiet time – slow and thoughtful, full of remembrance for the year that's been. In our weakness, we crave warmth, comfort, and understanding, until deep snows cover us completely and our year is at an end.

But will we awaken to a new spring? Will we feel a stirring in our souls, the warmth of reinvigoration, a sense of freedom and exhilaration at a new and miraculous start?

Religions speak of Heaven, Paradise, Nirvana, where life is eternal, and peace and love abound. Some speak of meeting loved ones who have gone before us to a place that is unchartered and ethereal. Others suggest reincarnation; that we are here on Earth to learn lessons, and we will return over and over, in different guises, until those lessons are learned.

But what if the planet itself, with its extraordinary seasons and cycles, were sacred? What if, every day, we walk on hallowed soil? What if the spirit present in every living thing were an integral part of a huge and magnificent whole, both divine and beautiful?

A sacred and universal energy flows through and around us all. We are interconnected, a part of each other, and a part of something unfathomable – greater and more majestic than we could ever imagine – consciousness everlasting; divine awareness; love supreme.

## STAR-DANCER

With your life complete
and your earthly deeds done,
we now return you
to All That Is,
you star-dancer, wind-rider,
wave-skimmer, sky-dreamer,
a living part of the universe,
ceaseless and unending.

Your energy, your spark
can never die.
You are dancing
with the playful breeze,
twirling, spinning
with the falling leaves,
bejewelled
with morning dew.

We give thanks for your life,
knowing that you are still close by,
and knowing we will find you
in the cooling summer rain,
in the greening of spring,
the darkening of winter,
the shifting tides of the sea.

And in each new day,
we will be grateful,
with each intake of breath,
for having known you,

for having loved you,
as we live on,
blessed by your memory,
lit by your sun.

## WHEN ALL IS THUNDER-BLACK

When all is thunder-black and constant night
and gladness is a half-held memory,
I shine upon you with my rainbow light.

If hope is gone and life a dismal plight,
open your shutters, set your white dove free,
when all is thunder-black and constant night.

On tempestuous grey, white wings gleam bright;
so know that, in your steep-plummeting sea,
I shine upon you with my rainbow light.

With a green twig of hope, I will alight
on your drowning ship tossed in misery,
when all is thunder-black and constant night.

Then I shall guide you to still mountain heights
and, comforted, you will be near to me,
as I shine on you with my rainbow light.

From here, the course you steer will be right
as you have come to know me and can see,
when all is thunder-black and constant night,
I shine upon you with my rainbow light.

## NOW THAT YOU'VE GONE

I've noticed I iron more. In smooth
hypnotic sweeps, I heat the cool white sheets;
I flatten them to pack-ice, wait
for them to melt. The rising steam
fills my lungs; makes me feel my breath.

The evening house has sounds.
The boiler's quick intake of breath
is your throat about to talk.
Even the indifferent fridge sighs.
Cooling pipes click your homecoming;
it's your key in the lock each time.
And I'm on my feet – transfixed –
till I see again I've been tricked.

Late in the garden, I watch
the rounded hedge – mangle-like –
catch and stretch shadows like wrung shirts
across your forsaken lawn. And
even opportunist dandelions
close tightly shut, for fear of losing
too much yellow. Now that you've gone.

## BLACKBIRD

It scared her to think, beyond
the glass, there was more.
This window was her world. Her globe
was twelve squares sliced
by lines of longitude and latitude.
A child again – Sunday-entrapped,
straining to peer through segments,
leaded and stained – she couldn't find
the whole picture.

The upper panels contained oak boughs,
swirling rooks in a sliver
of sky. The middle – a field corner,
brown-dotted with pheasant,
the cat's sometime hunting ground.
Below, trimmed hawthorn held
her favoured bird – the spry gentleman,
tail-coated for opera.

Long birdsung evenings
passed like summer cloud.
Leaves fell silent
as a vigil into russet-gold,
where they sepia-fixed
in winter's freeze,
only to thaw without her
the following spring.

And even now an aria
from her minstrel in mournful garb
can return me to that room,
that half-ghost time
and her window.

**AFON**

Nightfall,
and the moon blinks
through trailing cloud
to silver the meadow
and snaking stream.
The river's glinting thread
slips through silence –
a thin slither of mercury
to guide me home.

## BIOGRAPHY

**Patricia Sumner** worked as a teacher for ten years, specialising in English. She now runs her own writing, editing and proofreading business (pat-cilan.co.uk). She is also a children's author (mama-pat.com).

Pat has written and had published children's picture books, adventure stories and factual books, educational resources on creative writing, prize-winning poetry and plays.

She lives in beautiful North Wales with her husband, son and daughter, their pedigree RSD (Romanian street dog) and elderly ginger tom.

Printed in the UK
by
mixam.co.uk